THE
+ BIG +
COUNT
DOWN
× + = −

2.67 TRILLION INTERNET SEARCHES EACH YEAR USING TECHNOLOGY

PAUL MASON

W
FRANKLIN WATTS
LONDON • SYDNEY

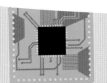

Franklin Watts
Published in paperback in Great Britain in 2020 by
The Watts Publishing Group
Copyright © The Watts Publishing Group, 2018

Editor: Julia Bird/Julia Adams
Design and illustration: Mark Ruffle
www.rufflebrothers.com

ISBN: 978 1 4451 6088 7

Photo credits: ALPHA PROD/Shutterstock: 18c
Tomasz Czajkowski/Shutterstock: 13b. Samy
Golay/TIPress/Getty Images: 15b. Edward Gooch/
Hulton Archive/Getty Images: 20b. guteksk7/
Shutterstock: 16cl. Elizaveta Kirina/Shutterstock: 27b.
KPG_Payless/Shutterstock: 14tl. Phil MacD Photo/
Shutterstock: 14tr. mandritoiu/Shutterstock: 14tc.
Marques/Shutterstock: front cover bc. Master Video/
Shutterstock: 25br. mezzotint/Shutterstock: 24cl.
Sergey Novikov/Shutterstock: front cover c. Vadim
Sadovski/Shutterstock (references from NASA): 28tr.
SpeedKingz/Shutterstock: front cover tr. Jack Taylor/
Getty Images: 16tl. Roger-Viollet/Getty Images: 26t.

Every attempt has been made to clear copyright.
Should there be any inadvertent omission
pleaseapply to the publisher for rectification.

Franklin Watts
An imprint of
Hachette Children's Group
Part of The Watts Publishing Group
Carmelite House
50 Victoria Embankment
London EC4Y 0DZ

An Hachette UK Company
www.hachette.co.uk
www.franklinwatts.co.uk

Printed in Dubai

Throughout the book you are given data relating to various pieces of information covering the topic. The numbers will most likely be an estimation based on research made over a period of time and in a particular area. Some other research may reach a different set of data, and all these figures may change with time as new research and information is gathered. The numbers provided within this book are believed to be correct at the time of printing and have been sourced from the following sites and organisations:

American Institute of Physics; American Journal of Epidemiology; *Auto Express* magazine; BBC; bicycling.com; BP; Carbon Brief online magazine; climate.nasa.gov; copyhackers.com; CNN; *Daily Telegraph*; The *Guardian*; International Energy Agency, internetlivestats.com; internetworldstats.com; Office of Energy Efficiency and Renewable Energy (www.energy.gov); malonemediagroup.com; NASA; ourworldindata.org; Pew Research; populationpyramid.net; Renewable Energy Policy Network for the 21st Century; sciencealert.com; Science Museum; searchengineland.com; spitfireperformance.com; statista.com; techcrunch.com; techterms.com; webcitation.org; World Bank; World Energy Council; United States Geological Survey; US Energy Information Administration.

CONTENTS

COUNTING DOWN TECHNOLOGY

Technology is scientific knowledge used for practical purposes. Even the simplest object is made using technology. A kitchen knife, for example, is made using the technologies of mining, steel production and metalwork.

MINING, STEEL PRODUCTION, METALWORK

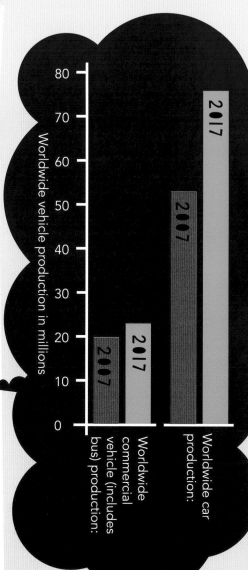

Worldwide vehicle production in millions

- 2017
- 2007
- 2017
- 2007

Worldwide commercial vehicle (includes bus) production:

Worldwide car production:

Technology surrounds us from the moment we wake up until we go to sleep again. At every stage of the day we come into contact with it:

07:30 ALARM
An alarm clock probably uses electronic technology, or maybe a phone jammed with computer technology wakes you.

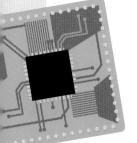

07:31 GET UP, BREAKFAST, SHOWER
If you turn on lights, they use electronic technology and are powered by energy technology. So are kettles for hot drinks and a hot shower.

08:00 CATCH BUS
Vehicle and energy technology are used in an actual bus, and construction technology in roads, bridges and tunnels.

08:45 SCHOOL
A school is built using construction technology, relies on energy to run and has computer-powered activities.

04:00 HOME TIME
The morning's technologies are repeated, maybe without the shower, but with some extra computing or games and media technology.

Since around 2000, the development of computers and the Internet has dramatically changed the world. Computers were once devices that people used as typewriters or calculators, but now they are machines that affect every part of our lives. The Internet has created a way for these machines to communicate.

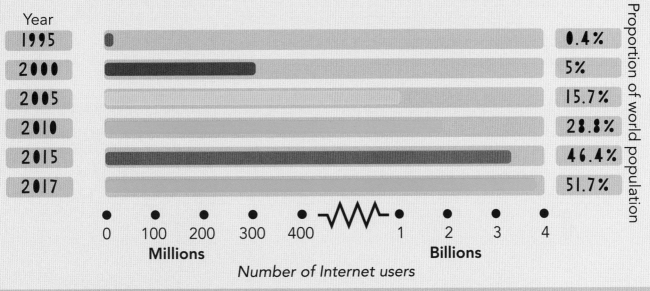

Year		Proportion of world population
1995		0.4%
2000		5%
2005		15.7%
2010		28.8%
2015		46.4%
2017		51.7%

0 100 200 300 400 1 2 3 4
Millions **Billions**
Number of Internet users

IN 2017, FOR THE FIRST TIME OVER HALF THE PEOPLE IN THE WORLD HAD ACCESS TO THE INTERNET.

TECHNOLOGY AND NUMBERS

Numbers are a crucial part of technology. Mathematics helps engineers design strong, safe bridges, skyscrapers, tunnels and other structures. In transport, numbers control everything from the speed needed for an airplane to take off to how often traffic lights should change.

This equation for working out lift shows that without numbers, turning science theory into technology would be impossible.

In technology, numbers start with **0**. Without the binary number system of **0s and 1s** (see p.16), computers could not work. There are other numbers so massive that people have had to invent new words for them. A **googol**, for example, is the number **1** followed by **100 zeroes**.

A (area) D (drag)
L (lift)
V (velocity)

$L = k V^2 A\, cl$
Each letter represents a number:
k is always 0.005
V is velocity (speed)
A is the wing area
cl is a measure of drag that depends on A

5

2,080,240,700,000 GOOGLE SEARCHES A YEAR

Many people use search-engine technology every day, often **more than once**. In a world with **7,600,000,000 people**, that means the most popular engines see a lot of traffic.

In 2018, Google was making **65,964** searches per second. That works out to be:
3,957,840 each minute, or …
237,470,400 every hour, or …
5,699,289,600 per day, or …
39,895,027,000 a week, or …
2,080,240,700,000 a year.

POPULAR SEARCH ENGINES

Google is easily the world's most popular search engine. It is used for more than **six times** as many searches as the next most used one, Baidu. Baidu is a Chinese search engine: in its home country it is used by **76% of people**. Next most popular are Bing and Yahoo. In 2018 these **four** were the only engines that powered more than **1%** of searches.

HOW SEARCH ENGINES WORK

Search engines work by sending out pieces of software called 'spiders' to collect information about websites. For example, the spiders might notice that a website uses lots of words and images connected to scooters. The information the spiders find is 'indexed', or turned into a list of where to find particular kinds of information. Then when someone searches for 'scooter', the engine knows which websites to suggest.

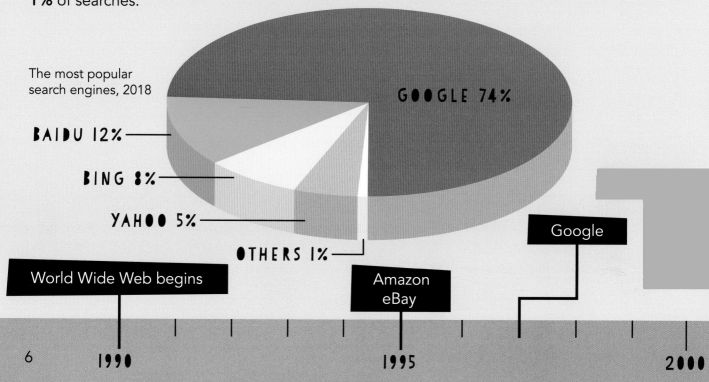

The most popular search engines, 2018

GOOGLE 74%

BAIDU 12%

BING 8%

YAHOO 5%

OTHERS 1%

World Wide Web begins

Amazon eBay

Google

1990

1995

2000

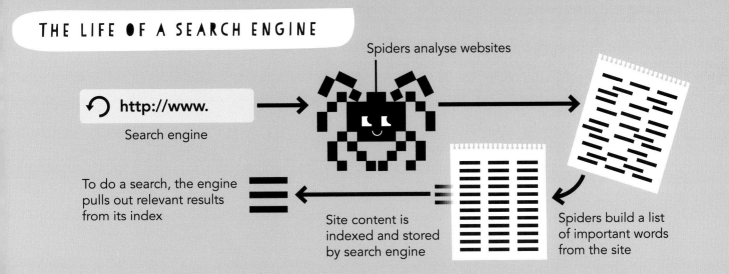

Spiders analyse websites

http://www.
Search engine

To do a search, the engine pulls out relevant results from its index

Site content is indexed and stored by search engine

Spiders build a list of important words from the site

INTERNET RICHES

The biggest Internet and computing companies were often started by **one person**, or just a small group of people. As the Internet has become more popular, these companies have increased massively in value. Their owners are now among the world's richest people.

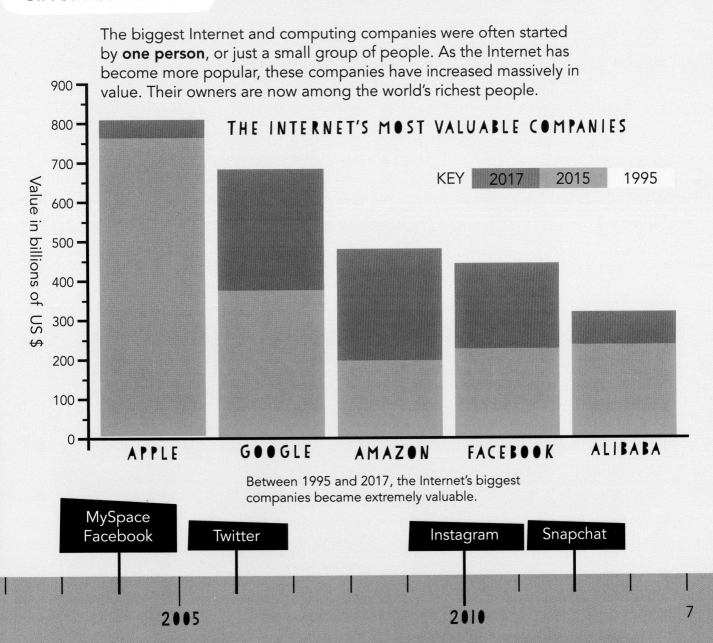

THE INTERNET'S MOST VALUABLE COMPANIES

KEY 2017 2015 1995

Value in billions of US $

900
800
700
600
500
400
300
200
100
0

APPLE   GOOGLE   AMAZON   FACEBOOK   ALIBABA

Between 1995 and 2017, the Internet's biggest companies became extremely valuable.

MySpace Facebook

Twitter

Instagram

Snapchat

2005   2010

132,763,000,000 TOE OF ENERGY USED BY THE WORLD EACH YEAR

One TOE is the amount of energy contained in a tonne of oil. At the moment, most of the world's energy technology uses oil and other fossil fuels.

WORLD ENERGY SOURCES

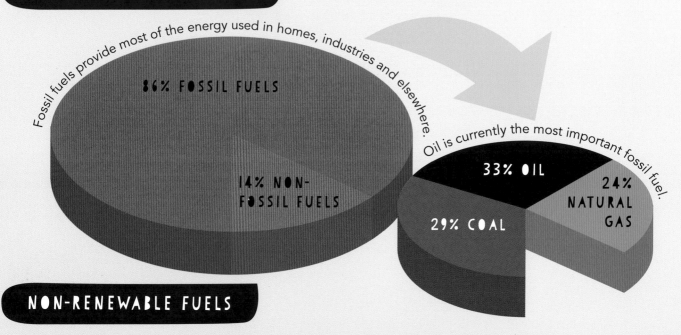

Fossil fuels provide most of the energy used in homes, industries and elsewhere.

86% FOSSIL FUELS

14% NON-FOSSIL FUELS

Oil is currently the most important fossil fuel.

33% OIL

24% NATURAL GAS

29% COAL

NON-RENEWABLE FUELS

Fossil fuels are made of the remains of plants and animals that lived **millions of years ago**. There is only a certain amount of each fossil fuel in the world, and **one day** they will run out. When this happens depends on:

- how much fossil fuel the world uses each year
- how much is left
- whether any more is found.

Because they will one day run out, fossil fuels are often called non-renewable.

WHEN WILL FOSSIL FUELS RUN OUT?

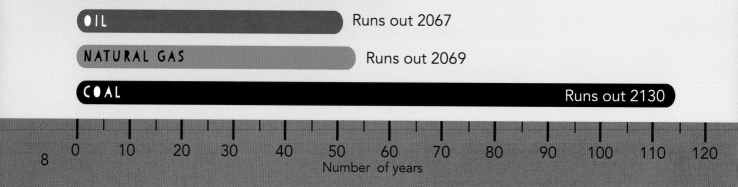

OIL   Runs out 2067

NATURAL GAS   Runs out 2069

COAL   Runs out 2130

| 0 | 10 | 20 | 30 | 40 | 50 | 60 | 70 | 80 | 90 | 100 | 110 | 120 |

Number of years

DAMAGE TO THE ENVIRONMENT

Fossil fuels harm the environment. When they are burned to make energy, carbon dioxide gas (CO_2) is released. It rises into Earth's atmosphere and joins a layer of greenhouse gases. (They have this name because they keep heat in the atmosphere). So much fossil fuel has now been burned that Earth's overall temperature is rising, a process called global warming.

ALTERNATIVE ENERGY SOURCES

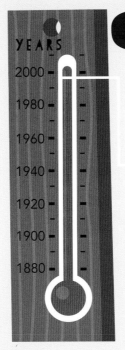

YEARS

2000

1980

1960

1940

1920

1900

1880

RISING TEMPERATURES

Global temperature records began in 1880:

- ☀ **17 out of the 18** warmest years have been since 2001
- ☀ **1** was in 1998
- ☀ **0** were in 1880–1997

Global warming has led to changes in the world's climate, with droughts, floods, rising sea levels and an increase in violent storms.

Around the world, new technologies are being developed to generate energy from renewable sources. These include solar, wind and hydroelectric (water) power. They do not rely on burning fossil fuels and do not affect the environment in the same way as traditional power sources.

RENEWABLE ENERGY TYPE	INCREASE 2011-16	INCREASE 2017-22
Wind	**285** Gigawatts	**321** Gigawatts
Solar	**260** Gigawatts	**438** Gigawatts
Hydropower	**215** Gigawatts	**199** Gigawatts
Others	**45** Gigawatts	**44** Gigawatts

1 GIGAWATT OF ENERGY IS:

... the amount produced by **2,000** Corvette Z06 supercars, or **12,500** Nissan Leaf electric cars ...

... as much as you get from **500** wind turbines, or **4,600,000** photovoltaic solar panels ...

X 12,500

X 500

X 100,000,000

... enough to power **100,000,000** LED bulbs.

Wind and solar energy are increasingly important as we aim to reduce the **132,763,000,000 TOE of fossil fuels** used annually. In **2011–16** they added **68%** of the extra energy from renewables. Between **2017** and **2022** they are expected to add at least **82%**.

6,100,000,000 SMARTPHONES IN USE BY 2020

Today smartphones outnumber traditional land-line phone connections for the first time.

This adds up to **0.79 smartphones** for every man, woman and child in the world.*

*Based on a projected 2020 world population of **7,760,000,000**

TOP 10 COUNTRIES BY NUMBER OF SMARTPHONE USERS

In 2017, these countries had the greatest numbers of smartphone users:

		MILLIONS OF USERS			MILLIONS OF USERS
1	China	**717.31**	6	Japan	**63.09**
2	India	**300.12**	7	Germany	**55.49**
3	USA	**226.29**	8	Indonesia	**54.49**
4	Brazil	**79.58**	9	Mexico	**52.99**
5	Russia	**78.36**	10	UK	**44.95**

PERCENTAGES OF SMARTPHONE USERS

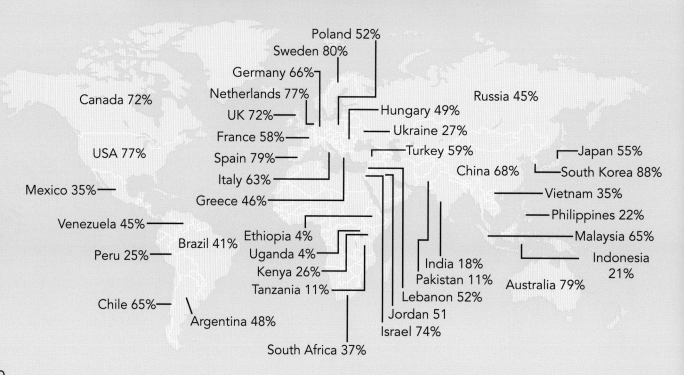

Poland 52%
Sweden 80%
Germany 66%
Netherlands 77%
UK 72%
France 58%
Spain 79%
Italy 63%
Greece 46%
Canada 72%
USA 77%
Mexico 35%
Venezuela 45%
Brazil 41%
Peru 25%
Chile 65%
Argentina 48%
Ethiopia 4%
Uganda 4%
Kenya 26%
Tanzania 11%
South Africa 37%
Hungary 49%
Ukraine 27%
Turkey 59%
India 18%
Pakistan 11%
Lebanon 52%
Jordan 51
Israel 74%
Russia 45%
China 68%
Japan 55%
South Korea 88%
Vietnam 35%
Philippines 22%
Malaysia 65%
Indonesia 21%
Australia 79%

HOW SMARTPHONES WORK

At the heart of a smartphone is a radio. The radio contacts a nearby antenna, sending and receiving signals. The signals contain data which the phone converts using processors and computer chips, which also allow it to run layers of software.

SOFTWARE STACK IN A TYPICAL SMARTPHONE

APPLICATIONS: tasks the phone does regularly, like displaying the menu screen

USER INTERFACE: the graphics and layouts you see on screen.

APPLICATION EXECUTION ENVIRONMENT (AEE): the parts of the phone's software that let it work with apps from other companies

MIDDLEWARE: the software that powers basic functions such as security, Internet browsing and sending messages

KERNEL: core software for the hardware (on/off buttons, etc.) and basic functions

Each layer in the stack relies on the ones below it. Without the kernel software, for example, none of the other layers could work.

OPERATING SYSTEMS

A smartphone's operating system is the software that lets it work.

There were originally lots of operating systems, but by 2017 there were really only **two**. Apple's iOS was in **14% of devices** and Android was in **85.9%**.

SMARTPHONES V. OTHER DEVICES

With **6,100,000,000 smartphones** in use today, they are easily the most popular device when compared to tablets and computers. In the USA, for example, among people who had all **three**:

80% of people used a smartphone every day

67% used a computer every day

16% used a tablet every day

In poorer communities around the world, many people only have access to the Internet via their smartphone.

SMARTPHONE SLEEP

One in three people with a smartphone admits that they wake up at night to check it. Over time, disturbed nights of sleep affect health and the ability to think clearly. Sleep experts recommend not having a smartphone in your bedroom, or at least turning it off.

3,696,000,000 PASSENGERS CARRIED BY PLANE IN A YEAR

Since 1970, the number of passengers carried by planes has grown rapidly. Part of the reason for this growth is aircraft technology. Modern planes can fit more passengers, and fly further, faster and more safely.

WORLDWIDE INCREASE IN AIRCRAFT PASSENGERS 1970-2016

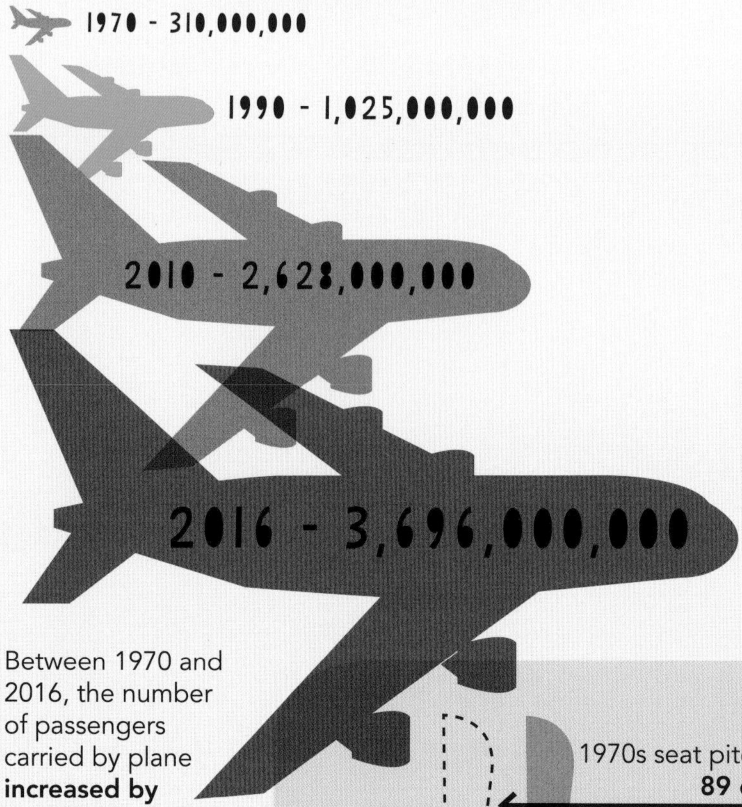

1970 - 310,000,000

1990 - 1,025,000,000

2010 - 2,628,000,000

2016 - 3,696,000,000

Between 1970 and 2016, the number of passengers carried by plane **increased by 1,192%** to **3,696,000,000 per year** in 2016.

CARBON FIBRE TECHNOLOGY

Aircraft are now built using carbon fibre instead of aluminium in much of their structure. Carbon fibre can be extremely light and strong. The lightness helps planes use less fuel.

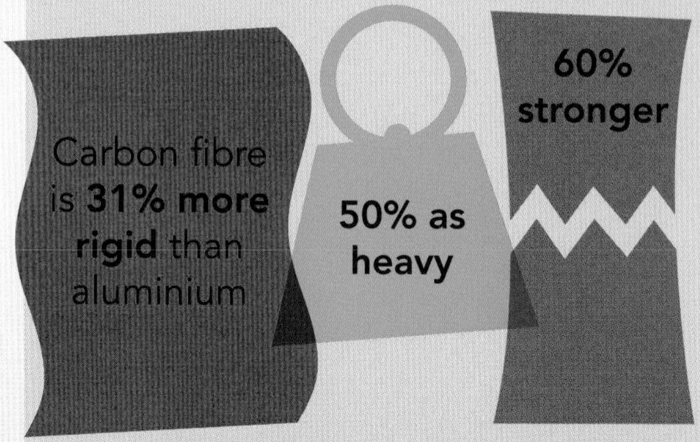

Carbon fibre is **31% more rigid** than aluminium

50% as heavy

60% stronger

Planes can also carry more passengers, partly because using lighter materials means they can be larger. The airline companies also allow less space per passenger, fitting more seats into their planes.

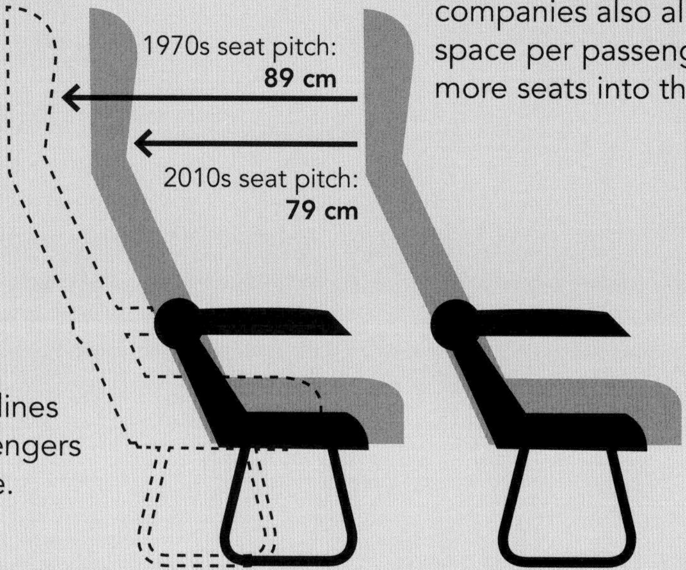

1970s seat pitch: **89 cm**

2010s seat pitch: **79 cm**

Today's airlines give passengers less space.

HOW DOES A JET ENGINE WORK?

Jet engines are fitted to most large aircraft. They work by using a fan to suck in air at the front of the engine. Inside is a compressor, which squeezes the air into a tighter space. The compressed air is mixed with fuel and set alight. As it fires out of the back of the engine, the plane is pushed forwards.

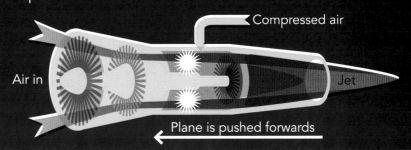

Compressed air

Air in

Jet

Plane is pushed forwards

LIFT

No plane could fly without lift. Lift is a force generated when an object and a fluid move past each other. When the object (e.g. a plane wing) forces the fluid (e.g. air) to change direction, it creates lift. Higher speeds create more lift. Most passenger planes need to be travelling at **250 kph** or more to take off.

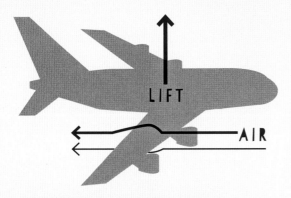

LIFT

AIR

PLANE POLLUTION

Jet aircraft release CO_2 (see page 9) high into the atmosphere. It quickly joins the layer of greenhouse gases that is trapping heat and thereby warming the planet. Each plane's vapour trail also contributes to global warming.

HOW FAST AIRCRAFT FLY

Tiger moth military and civilian biplane
257 kph

Apache attack helicopter
284 kph

Corvus Racer 540 acrobatics/air race plane
450 kph

Spitfire Second World War fighter
560 kph

Hercules military transport plane
570 kph

Airbus 380 passenger plane
1,020 kph

MiG-25 Foxbat fighter/interceptor
3,950 kph

300,000,000 METRES OF WIRE IN THE AKASHI KAIKYŌ BRIDGE

The Akashi Kaikyō has the longest span of any suspension bridge. A bridge this long – like the tallest skyscrapers and longest tunnels – is only possible because of modern construction technology.

RECORD-BREAKING SUSPENSION BRIDGES

	YEAR	NAME	CROSSING	CENTRAL SPAN
1.	1964	Verrazano Bridge	Staten Island and Brooklyn, USA	1.298 m
2.	1981	Humber Bridge	Humber Estuary between Lincolnshire and Yorkshire, UK	1,410 m
3.	1998	Akashi Kaikyō Bridge	Akashi Strait between the islands of Honshu and Awaji, Japan	1,991 m
4.	2022 (estimated)	Çanakkale 1915 Bridge	Dardanelles Strait between Europe and Asia	2,023 m

286 KPH

Wind speed the Akashi Kaikyō Bridge can withstand. It can also stand through earthquakes of up to 8.5 on the Richter Scale.

HOW IS A SUSPENSION BRIDGE BUILT?

Suspension bridges need strong foundations. Once these are in place, towers are built. Cables are strung between them. More cables are hung down from these linking cables: they hold up the bridge's road or rail track. Almost all suspension bridges also have supports called trusses underneath them.

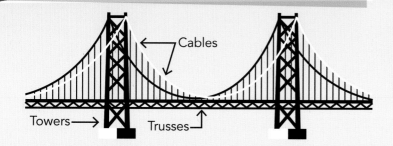

Cables

Towers →

Trusses

SKYSCRAPERS

Skyscrapers could not exist without **two crucial technologies**: concrete and steel. A skyscraper rests on concrete bases. On top of these are crisscrossed steel girders, called a grillage. The grillage supports the steel skeleton of the skyscraper. Everything else – the walls and floor of the skyscraper – is supported by this skeleton.

THE TALLEST TOWER

In 2010, the Burj Khalifa in Dubai took the record for the world's tallest building – but plans have been developed for at least **four skyscrapers** that may be even taller.

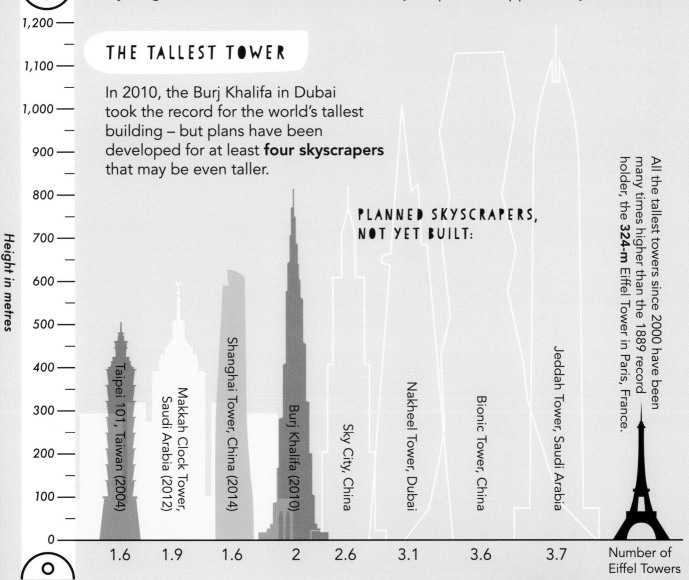

Height in metres

1,200
1,100
1,000
900
800
700
600
500
400
300
200
100
0

PLANNED SKYSCRAPERS, NOT YET BUILT:

Taipei 101, Taiwan (2004)
Makkah Clock Tower, Saudi Arabia (2012)
Shanghai Tower, China (2014)
Burj Khalifa (2010)
Sky City, China
Nakheel Tower, Dubai
Bionic Tower, China
Jeddah Tower, Saudi Arabia

All the tallest towers since 2000 have been many times higher than the 1889 record holder, the **324-m** Eiffel Tower in Paris, France.

| 1.6 | 1.9 | 1.6 | 2 | 2.6 | 3.1 | 3.6 | 3.7 | Number of Eiffel Towers |

LONG-HAUL TUNNELS

Long tunnels have been made possible by modern technology. Special tunnel-boring machines with huge cutting heads dig the tunnel automatically. It is usually then lined with concrete for strength. This is how mega-tunnels such as the Gotthard Base Tunnel and Channel Tunnel were built. The world's longest transport tunnels carry trains. For cars, the risk of accidents, breaking down or dangerous pollution is too high.

57 km
Length of the world's longest rail tunnel, Gotthard Base Tunnel in Switzerland.

75,000,000 BYTES IN A SONG

A byte is a unit of computer memory, usually made up of **eight 'bits'**. A bit is either a **one or a zero**, so a byte is a sequence of **eight ones and zeros**, for example: **10101101**.

HALF A BYTE, OR 4 BITS, IS KNOWN AS A NIBBLE.

Colossus, the first programmable electronic digital computer (above), and an iPad!

WHAT ARE BYTES FOR?

Computers originally used bytes to process letters. Each letter was given a number in binary, a number system that uses only **0s and 1s**. Computers can process binary – their electronic systems understand the numbers as either 'off' or 'on'.

+ ● BINARY ALPHABET ◀ ▶ ● ○

a	01100001	j	01101010	s	01110011
b	01100010	k	01101011	t	01110100
c	01100011	l	01101100	u	01110101
d	01100100	m	01101101	v	01110110
e	01100101	n	01101110	w	01110111
f	01100110	o	01101111	x	01111000
g	01100111	p	01110000	y	01111001
h	01101000	q	01110001	z	01111010
i	01101001	r	01110010		

These are the bytes for small letters. Capital letters have a whole new set of bytes; so do numbers, punctuation marks and so on.

+ ● TAKE THE BINARY CHALLENGE: ◀ ▶ ● ●

01101101   01100001   01110100   01101000   01110011

01110010   01101101   01101100   01101101   01110011

What do the numbers say? The answer is on page 32.

FORMATS

Each binary number can have more than **one meaning**, depending on the format it is recorded in. So **01100001** can be not only the letter 'a', but also the number **97**, a colour in a video or a sound in a recording. There are different formats for text, images, audio and video.

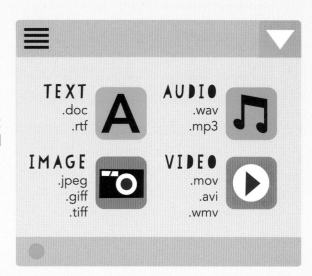

TEXT
.doc
.rtf

AUDIO
.wav
.mp3

IMAGE
.jpeg
.giff
.tiff

VIDEO
.mov
.avi
.wmv

TOO MANY BYTES

Try writing out your name in binary code. After **just two or three words**, you already have a long string of numbers. Imagine how many would be in a book, which is a relatively small computer file. As computers started to do more complicated tasks, the numbers they had to deal with started to get really big. New names were needed for the numbers of bytes in a file:

kilobyte (kB) = **1,024 bytes** (or about **8,192 bits**. Or **4,096 nibbles**)

megabyte (MB) = **1,048,576 bytes**

gigabyte (GB) = **1,073,741,824 bytes**

terrabyte (TB) = **1,099,511,627,776 bytes**

petabyte (PB) = **1,125,899,906,842,624 bytes**

exabyte (EB) = **1,152,921,504,606,846,976 bytes**

Everything said by all humans, ever, is sometimes said to be about **5 exabytes of information**.

FILE SIZES

Bytes are used to record all kinds of information on a computer. The smallest files are simple text ones. Files with videos and sound are much bigger - for example a song file contains around **75,000,000 bytes**. Interactive files such as games are even larger.

TYPICAL FILE SIZES

14-line email
14 KB

eBook
2.6 MB

Single 50-minute box-set episode
1 GB

Every word spoken by someone by the time they are 25
1 TB

All data on the Internet in the year 2000
1 PB

20,000 GAUSS MAGNET IN THE MOST POWERFUL MRI SCANNERS

A gauss is a unit of magnetic force: more gauss = stronger force. Magnetic Resonance Imaging (MRI) scanners are used to make an image of the inside of a body.

A magnet is anything that has a magnetic force. It pulls some metal objects towards it, and either pulls at other magnets or pushes them away.

MAGNETIC POWER

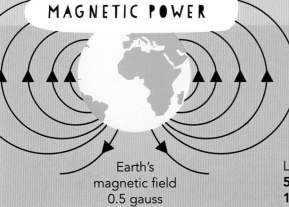

Earth's magnetic field
0.5 gauss

Low-power MRI scanner
5,000 gauss
10,000 x Earth's magnetic field

Most powerful MRI scanner
20,000 gauss
40,000 x Earth's magnetic field

MRI SCANNERS

MRI scanners allow doctors to see what's going on inside a patient without cutting them open.

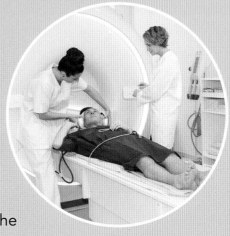

The magnets in the scanner cause almost all the hydrogen atoms in the patient's body to line up with the magnetic field.

A strong radio pulse, aimed only at the hydrogen atoms, gets different responses depending on what kind of tissue it reaches.

The computer converts these responses into an image of the inside of the body.

LOOKING INSIDE PATIENTS

900 CE
Al-Zahrawi publishes a medical book called *An Aid for Those Who Lack the Capacity to Read Big Books.* His descriptions of surgery become popular among doctors.

1800s
Anaesthetic that makes the patient unconscious allows surgeons to dig deeper into the human body.

1895
William Roentgen discovers X-rays, which can be used to take pictures of people's bones.

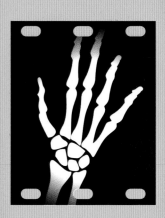

CHANGING TECHNOLOGY

Medical technologies have changed a lot over the last **100 years**. As a result, more people stay alive, and for longer, today than ever before. **Two** of the most important changes in medical technology are:

VACCINATION

Vaccination is a way of preventing disease by injecting people with a safe version of it. Their bodies learn how to produce antibodies to fight the disease.

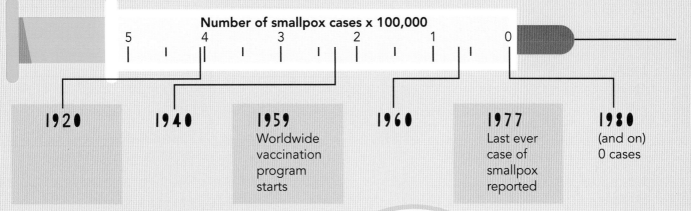

Number of smallpox cases x 100,000

5   4   3   2   1   0

1920

1940

1959
Worldwide vaccination program starts

1960

1977
Last ever case of smallpox reported

1980
(and on)
0 cases

STEM-CELL RESEARCH

Stem cells are cells that can change into another kind of cell. Today, scientists are trying to work out how to use them to replace damaged cells. For example, if the cells in someone's eye, ear or even their spinal cord are damaged, stem cells could be used to repair them.

1940s
Availability of antibiotics makes surgery safer, as fewer people die of infections.

1950s
Ultrasound is developed as a way of using sound waves to see inside a patient.

1972
Computerised Tomography (CT) is invented. CT scans produce a picture of a 'slice' of someone's body, but produce harmful radiation.

1970s
MRI scans are developed as a form of scan that does not harm the patient.

900% INCREASE IN CLICKS BECAUSE OF THE CURIOSITY GAP

NEWS SOURCES

The curiosity gap is the gap between what you know and what you'd like to know. It is one of the ways online news and media websites get you to click on a story.

In 2017, one survey found that increasing numbers of people look for news online, instead of on TV or the radio, or in newspapers.

TV
2016 **57%**
2017 **50%**

THE INTERNET
2016 **38%**
2017 **42%**

RADIO
2016 **25%**
2017 **25%**

PRINT NEWSPAPERS
2016 **20%**
2017 **18%**

THE CURIOSITY GAP IN ACTION

In TV shows, you experience the curiosity gap when adverts come on at an exciting moment. You want to know what happens next, so you wait for the show to begin again.

On the Internet, headline writers use the curiosity gap to get you to click and find out more. In one study this increased people's interest by **nine times or 900%**. Here are some examples:

THIS MOTHER OF FIVE FORCED EVERY MAN IN THE COUNTRY TO LISTEN TO HER

The campaign for women's suffrage (the right to vote in elections), led by Emmeline Pankhurst, is successful in Britain.

THIS WEEDY TEENAGER BECAME EUROPE'S MOST NOTORIOUS KILLER

Gavrilo Princip assassinates Archduke Franz Ferdinand, triggering the First World War.

THIS DIRTBAG DOCTOR'S MESS CHANGED MEDICINE FOREVER

Alexander Fleming discovers penicillin, leading to the development of antibiotics.

THEY THOUGHT IT WAS A REGULAR SUNDAY – BUT THEIR WORLD WAS ABOUT TO CHANGE FOREVER

Japanese planes launch a surprise attack on Pearl Harbor, Hawaii.

How a headline using the curiosity gap to get your attention might be written

Actual historical events

VIRAL STORIES

If enough people click on a story (or a video, quiz, etc.) then share it, it goes viral. The technology works in **two main ways**: through the 'Like' button or the 'Share' button.

If you hit 'Like' on a story – for example on Facebook – the site's algorithm records this, then tells the person who wrote the story plus some or all of your friends. If you click 'Share' you can choose what to say about a story, and sometimes who you share it with, as well as how it is shared (within the app, by email, for example).

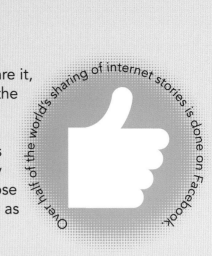

Over half of the worlds sharing of internet stories is done on Facebook.

MOST SHARED CONTENT ON FACEBOOK, 2017

'Despacito' by Luis Fonsi (music video, Spanish)

'Shape of You' by Ed Sheeran (music video, English)

Linkin Park Singer Dies (news item)

Quiz: Only **1 in 50 People** Identify These **16** Grammar Mistakes

'I've Been Crying' by Prue Nakarin (music video, Thai)

0 1 2 3 4 5 6 7 8 9 10 11 12 13 14 15 16 17 18 19 20 21 22 23

Most-shared content on Facebook x 1,000,000

SOCIAL WEBSITE/APP USE

In a 2018 survey, people were asked which websites and apps they used most and how often each day they visited them.

	Several times a day	About once a day	Less often	Daily user total
FACEBOOK	51%	23%	26%	74%
SNAPCHAT	49%	14%	36%	63%
INSTAGRAM	38%	22%	39%	60%
TWITTER	26%	20%	53%	46%
YOUTUBE	29%	17%	55%	45%

430 KPH SPEED OF THE FASTEST PASSENGER TRAIN

The fastest passenger train is the Shanghai Maglev. It takes just over **seven minutes** to travel **30.5 km** between Longyang Metro Station and Shanghai International Airport.

The fastest train so far – the L0 Maglev – reached **603 kph** at a test track in Japan in 2015.

WHAT IS MAGLEV?

Maglev is short for magnetic levitation. Maglev trains use two sets of magnets. **One set** pushes the train up into the air, so that it hovers above the track. The **second set** pushes the train along.

Maglev trains can reach high speeds because they are not slowed down by friction between wheels and track. The trains are also able to speed up and slow down much more quickly than normal ones.

OPERATING SPEEDS OF THE WORLD'S THREE FASTEST PASSENGER TRAINS.

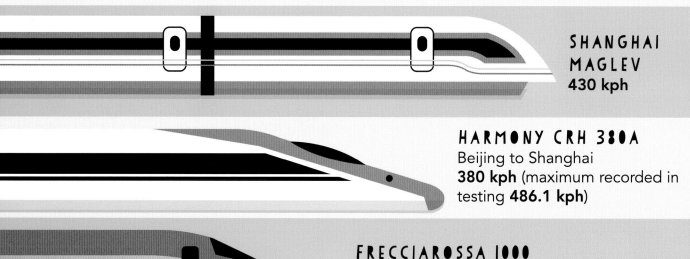

SHANGHAI MAGLEV
430 kph

HARMONY CRH 380A
Beijing to Shanghai
380 kph (maximum recorded in testing **486.1 kph**)

FRECCIAROSSA 1000
Milan to Rome
360 kph
(maximum recorded in testing **393.8 kph**).

ELECTRIC PERSONAL VEHICLES

Many vehicles now use electricity for power instead of fossil fuels. Even Formula 1 cars get part of their power from electric motors: they capture energy when the car brakes and store it in an electric battery.

Relative power

5 kph

EDISON ELECTRIC CAR, 1910s
Power: not known
For a short while, Edison and Ford (who had once worked for him) aimed to produce an electric car.

19 kph

ELECTRIC MILK FLOAT, 1931*
Power: **0.75 bhp** (brake horsepower)
Used in the UK for silent milk deliveries early in the mornings from the 1930s to the 1990s.

40 kph

HUMMINGBIRD LONDON TAXI, 1897
Power: **15 bhp** (estimated)
Built by Walter C Bersey, Queen Victoria was still on the throne when these electric taxis appeared on the streets of London.

VESPA ELETTRICA, 2018
Power: **5.4 bhp**
The first electric scooter from one of the first scooter manufacturers, the Elettrica has similar performance to a **50 cc** motor scooter.

55 kph

(estimated)

135 kph

RENAULT ZOE, 2012
Power: **87 bhp**
This small all-electric car has similar power to similar small petrol-powered cars.

TESLA MODEL S, 2012
Power: **779 bhp**
One of the fastest-accelerating cars in the world, in 'Ludicrous' mode the Model S can reach **100 kph** in **2.3 seconds**.

250 kph

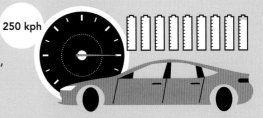

300+ kph

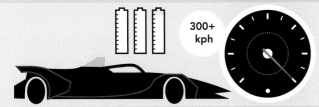

GEN2 FORMULA E RACER, 2018
Power: **335 bhp**
The car's performance in races is limited to a power of **270 bhp** and speeds of **280 kph**.

*Figures are for a 1931 Lewis Electruks, which was common in London; later milk floats were faster and more powerful.

134 MONTHS TO DO A (ROBOT) MARATHON ON MARS

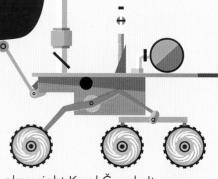

It was slow, but Mars-exploration robot 'Opportunity' didn't do badly. **First**, it was only designed to be active for **three months**. **Second**, it did complete the only off-Earth marathon (over a period of **134 months**).

'Robot' was first used by the Czech playwright Karel Čapek. It comes from an old word meaning 'forced to do boring work'.

ROBOTS

Robots are machines that can carry out complicated actions. Today robots are everywhere. They are used in factories, on battlefields, in the air, in people's homes and even on the roads.

Once a robotic camera drone has locked on to its target, it can follow it without being steered by a human.

VEHICLE PRODUCTION TIME

Robots have been used in vehicle manufacture since the 1960s. They do metal-cutting and pressing, welding, positioning of major parts (such as the engine) and painting.

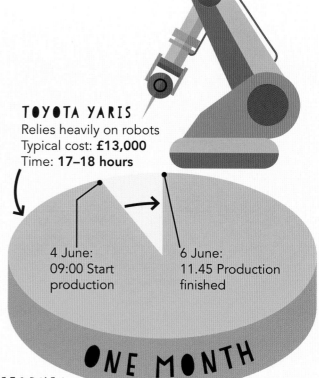

TOYOTA YARIS
Relies heavily on robots
Typical cost: **£13,000**
Time: **17–18 hours**

4 June: 09:00 Start production

22 June: 17:00 Production finished

ONE MONTH

4 June: 09:00 Start production

6 June: 11.45 Production finished

ONE MONTH

FERRARI CALIFORNIA
Some robots, mostly hand-built
Typical cost: **£155,000**
Time: 105 hours

ROBOT WORKERS

When industries start to use robots, it almost always means there are fewer jobs for humans. For the people who still have jobs, wages usually fall. Based on research in the USA:

Each robot in a workplace reduces the number of jobs for humans by **4.6 workers**.

THE UNITED STATE OF AMERICA
ONE DOLLAR

Introducing **one robot per 1,000 workers** reduces wages by **0.25–0.5%**.

ROBOT ACCIDENTS

The first accidental killing of a human by a robot happened in 1981, when a Japanese worker was crushed by a manufacturing robot. Today, robots can be equipped with motion and pressure sensors and cameras so they work safely alongside humans. Even so, accidents still happen. In 2018, a woman died after being hit by a robot car in Arizona, USA.

ROBOT CARS

Robot cars are also called 'self-driving cars' or 'autonomous vehicles'. They use several different technologies:

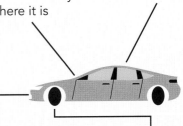

Mapping computers tell the car exactly where it is

Sensors detect the car's surroundings and other moving objects nearby

The car's computer uses object-recognition software

Steering and speed are adapted according to these inputs

The first 'home' robots were vacuum cleaners that appeared in the 1980s.

MEDICAL ROBOTS

In medicine, robot technology is being used in lots of different ways. Robot carts deliver supplies around hospitals, following a magnetic track. Robots are used to draw blood and perform surgery (under the control of a human surgeon). There have even been experiments with micro-bots – tiny robots less than **1 mm in diameter,** which swim through the blood to deliver drugs exactly where they are needed.

The da Vinci surgical system is powered by robotic technology.

24 GEARS ON A RACING BIKE

On modern racing bikes, the riders can shift gear by pressing a button. A signal goes down a wire to a derailleur, which changes gear for them.

In 1903 the first Tour de France racers had only **two gears**. To change gear they had to take the wheel out of the frame, and turn it round to a different-sized sprocket.

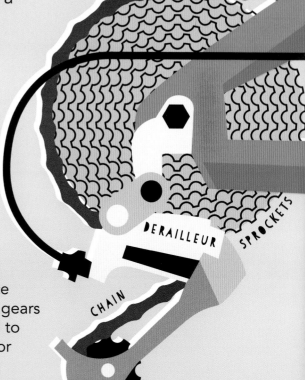

DERAILLEURS AND GEAR PERCENTAGES

A derailleur moves a bicycle's chain between gears. Once derailleurs were introduced in the 1930s, the number of gears on bikes went up and up. Eventually it began to be hard to work out how many gears a bike needed and how hard or easy they would be to pedal. To solve this, bike-makers came up with the idea of gear percentages.

TYPICAL GEAR PERCENTAGES ON A MOUNTAIN BIKE

The percentage is worked out by dividing the number of teeth on a sprocket (for example, **16**) by the number on the smallest sprocket (**10**), then multiplying by **100**. So, (16÷10) x 100 = 160%.

10-tooth sprocket. This is the starting point: **100%.**

12-tooth

14-tooth

16-tooth

18-tooth

21-tooth

24-tooth

28-tooth

32-tooth

36-tooth

42-tooth

50-tooth

CARBON FIBRE

Most bicycle frames are made out of metal or carbon fibre. Carbon fibre was first developed in the 1960s for use in aircraft. It is produced by making cloth from tiny threads of (mostly) carbon atoms. The cloth is then shaped and soaked with liquid resin. When the resin dries, the hard material that results is light and very strong.

VERY LITTLE OF THE WORLD'S CARBON FIBRE IS USED TO MAKE BIKES:

3 Boeing 737s
A Boeing 737 weighs about **42,000 kg** and carries **170 people**

=

Carbon fibre in all the bikes made in the world each year.
A typical carbon-fibre bike weighs about **9 kg** and carries **one person.**

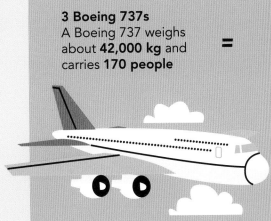

BICYCLE USE

Bicycles are a popular way of getting around. The technology they use is simple, bikes are cheap to buy and run, and they are easily repaired. In many countries, bicycle use is increasing. Bike-sharing schemes have made riding easier for people who do not own a bike. They use mobile-phone and Internet technology to borrow a bike for a limited time.

Number of cities worldwide offiering bike-share facilities

1000, 900, 800, 700, 600, 500, 400, 300, 200, 100, 0

2001 2002 2003 2004 2005 2006 2007 2008 2009 2010 2011 2012 2013 2014
Year

CHINA

China makes most of the world's bikes (about **60% of them**). China used to be famous as a place where far more people rode bicycles than drove cars. Today, bike use is falling in China, and city roads are increasingly congested with cars and other vehicles.

As Chinese people cycle less than before, huge piles of abandoned bikes like these have become a common sight.

I INTERNATIONAL SPACE STATION

The International Space Station (ISS) is loaded with technology to help astronauts survive in space. It is the only place outside Earth's atmosphere where humans live.

ISS is in orbit about **400 km** above Earth's surface. Aboard, the space station is separated into a US-led side and a Russian side. There is about as much space as inside a Boeing 747 aeroplane.

The controls of the Soyuz spacecraft, used to travel to the ISS, are in Russian – so the crew have to know Russian!

RELATIVE SPACE STATION SIZES

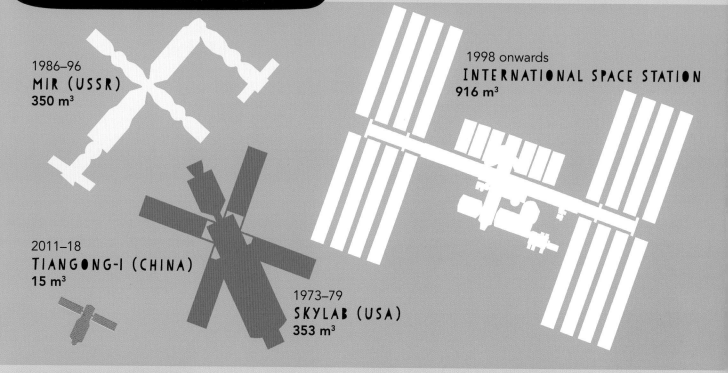

1986–96
MIR (USSR)
350 m³

1998 onwards
INTERNATIONAL SPACE STATION
916 m³

2011–18
TIANGONG-I (CHINA)
15 m³

1973–79
SKYLAB (USA)
353 m³

SKY(LAB) FALL

In 1979, the US space station Skylab's orbiting speed began to slow down. It was no longer travelling fast enough to resist Earth's gravity, so it began to fall back towards the surface. Fortunately Skylab mostly broke up on re-entry. A few pieces did reach Earth's surface, but did not harm anyone.

HOW LONG IS AN ISS DAY?

The answer to this depends on what you mean by a day. If it's **24 hours**, then a day is the same on ISS as on Earth. If you mean how long between sunrises, the answer is a bit more complicated:

ISS travels at **28,164 kph** and covers **675,924 km** every **24 hours**.

This means the space station orbits the Earth (and the Sun reappears in its windows) once every **1.5 hours**.

On average, the time between sunrise and sunset is **45 minutes**.

The crew sees **16 sunrises and sunsets** every **24 hours.**

EATING AND SLEEPING

With a sunrise every **90 minutes**, it can be hard for the astronauts to know when to eat and sleep. Alarms and timers warn them when they should prepare food, enter one of the tiny sleeping capsules, or just tie themselves to a wall for a nap*.

In its first **15 years**, astronauts ate about **26,500** meals aboard the ISS.

The maximum ISS crew size is **6**. That's the most people the escape systems can handle if something goes wrong.

THE ISS HAS A MASS OF 417 TONNES, WHICH IS ABOUT THE SAME AS:

32% OF A GIANT REDWOOD (1,300 TONNES)

66% OF RIO DE JANEIRO'S CHRIST THE REDEEMER STATUE (635 TONNES)

4 X BLUE WHALE (105 TONNES)

65 X TYRANNOSAURUS REX (6.4 TONNES)

*Astronauts do not feel gravity aboard ISS: unless they tie themselves down they will float off.

FURTHER INFORMATION

BOOKS
Infographic How It Works: Today's Technology by Jon Richards and Ed Simkins (Wayland, 2016)

If: A Mind-Bending Way of Looking at Big Ideas and Numbers by David J. Smith (Wayland, 2016)

STEM-gineers: Triumphs of Technology by Rob Colson (Wayland, 2018)

How They Made Things Work (series) by Richard Platt and David Lawrence (Franklin Watts, 2018)

WEBSITES
A one-stop shop for just about everything you could want to know about space technology: **www.nasa.gov/kidsclub/index.html**

For a fun, interactive site that pops up some interesting facts about engineering as you click your mouse across the screen: **egfi-k12.org**

If you want to try your hand at coding or find out more about computers, head to: **code.org**

Note to parents and teachers: Every effort has been made by the publisher to ensure that these websites contain no inappropriate or offensive material. However, because of the nature of the Internet, it is impossible to guarantee that the content of these sites will not be altered. We strongly advise that Internet access is supervised by a responsible adult.

LARGE NUMBERS

1,000,000,000,000,000,000,000,000,000,000,000 = ONE DECILLION

1,000,000,000,000,000,000,000,000,000,000 = ONE NONILLION

1,000,000,000,000,000,000,000,000,000 = ONE OCTILLION

1,000,000,000,000,000,000,000,000 = ONE SEPTILLION

1,000,000,000,000,000,000,000 = ONE SEXTILLION

1,000,000,000,000,000,000 = ONE QUINTILLION

1,000,000,000,000,000 = ONE QUADRILLION

1,000,000,000,000 = ONE TRILLION

1,000,000,000 = ONE BILLION

1,000,000 = ONE MILLION

1000 = ONE THOUSAND

100 = ONE HUNDRED

10 = TEN

1 = ONE

GLOSSARY

algorithm	set of rules followed by a computer
anaesthetic	drug used to stop a patient feeling any pain
antibiotic	drug used to prevent or cure an infection
antibody	part of blood that fights disease
atom	smallest part of a chemical that can exist, so small that it cannot be seen
bhp	short for brake horsepower, a unit of measurement for power. One bhp equals 0.7457 kW
binary	number system using only the numbers 0 and 1
computer chip	small electronic unit that helps computers deal with information and remember things
congested	crowded or very busy
cutting head	part of a machine – especially a tunnelling machine – that cuts into rock or soil
derailleur	flexible 'arm' that a cyclist uses to move a bike chain from one gear to another
fluid	matter that does not have a fixed shape. Fluids can be liquids such as water, or gases such as oxygen
force	a push or a pull
format	way in which information, particularly computerised information, is organised
foundation	base on which a building or other kind of structure rests
friction	force of resistance that happens when matter rubs against other matter
girder	large metal beam that is used to make a structure stronger
hydroelectric	using the power of water flowing downhill to generate electricity
levitation	act of moving upward to hover in the air without any visible support
mass	amount of matter an object contains
orbit	repeated path around an object – for example, Earth orbits the Sun and the Moon orbits Earth
photovoltaic	using sunlight to make electricity
pressing	forcing metal into a new shape by pressing it against a form (a solid object in the shape you want the metal to be)
processor	machine that performs a series of steps or operations to do a particular job. This word is often used for the 'central processing unit' of a computer
renewable	able to be replaced with more of the same thing
resin	sticky liquid that goes hard when it dries
Richter Scale	measure of the strength of an earthquake
search engine	computer system that is designed to find information on the Internet
sensor device	device for detecting something, such as movement or light
software	computer code written to do a particular job
spinal cord	string of nerves running from the brain down through the backbone
sprocket	toothed wheel that grips on to a bicycle chain
survey	set of questions that aims to find out what people think about a subject
tissue	any of the kinds of material animals and plants are made of, for example bone, flesh, wood, etc.
truss	framework designed to support something, for example a roof
USSR	short for the Union of Soviet Socialist Republics, a country with Russia at its heart that existed from 1922 to 1991
vapour trail	line of water left behind by aircraft, which looks like a white streak in the sky
viral	on the Internet, this means spreading rapidly and to a lot of computers
welding	joining together pieces of metal by heating them

INDEX